# OXFORD
# First Book
## of
# Art

# OXFORD
# First Book
# of
# Art

## Gillian Wolfe

# OXFORD
UNIVERSITY PRESS

# OXFORD
## UNIVERSITY PRESS

Great Clarendon Street, Oxford OX2 6DP

Oxford University Press is a department of the University of Oxford.
It furthers the University's objective of excellence in research, scholarship,
and education by publishing worldwide in

Oxford  New York

Athens  Auckland  Bangkok  Bogotá  Buenos Aires  Calcutta
Cape Town  Chennai  Dar es Salaam  Delhi  Florence  Hong Kong  Istanbul
Karachi  Kuala Lumpur  Madrid  Melbourne  Mexico City  Mumbai
Nairobi  Paris  São Paulo  Singapore  Taipei  Tokyo  Toronto  Warsaw

with associated companies in  Berlin  Ibadan

Oxford is a registered trade mark of Oxford University Press
in the UK and in certain other countries

© Gillian Wolfe 1999

The moral rights of the author have been asserted

First published in hardback 1999
First published in paperback 2000

British Library Cataloguing in Publication Data available

ISBN 0-19-910760 2

1 3 5 7 9 10 8 6 4 2

Designed by White Design
Printed in Spain

Reclining Figure,
1951, *by Henry
Moore*

# Contents

How to use this book                    6

Mother and Child                        8

Faces                                  10

Figures                                12

Moving Figures                         14

Working                                16

Relaxing                               18

Animals                                20

Imagined Creatures                     22

Spring and Summer                      24

Autumn and Winter                      26

Light and Shade                        28

Music                                  30

Dance                                  32

Shapes                                 34

Patterns                               36

Letters and Numbers                    38

That's Strange                         40

Art Detective Quiz                     42

Picture List                           44

Index                                  47

# How to use this book

In this book there are paintings, drawings, weavings and sculptures.

Some of them were made a long time ago,

and some were made quite recently.

They come from all around the world,

and were made by artists of all kinds. But when these artists were children they drew and made imaginative art – just like you!

The pictures in the book are grouped together under headings, so that you can see how different artists have made pictures about a particular topic.

You can find out about each picture by reading the description next to it.

## Mother and Child

The Naughty Boy, by Hubert von Herkomer

A pretty country cottage, overgrown with roses and creepers, is the background for a family scene. An **angry** mother lifts up her *naughty* boy, and her head is turned away as she furiously tells someone behind her what he has done. The little boy looks uncomfortable as he is held roughly under the arms. Neither of them looks happy.

The infant Jesus is **frightened** by a fluttering bird, which young St John holds out to him. He turns to his mother Mary for comfort. The scene is carved out of a stone called marble, but the artist did not finish it. Can you see where Michelangelo's chisel cut the stone *roughly* at the outer edges? He then used a smaller chisel to chip *d e l i c a t e l y* at the figures.

Madonna and Child, by Michelangelo Buonarroti

This artist loved to paint mothers with their children. She captured their most **tender** moments together. Bath-time is ordinary and everyday, yet here we feel that we are allowed to *p e e p* in on an especially private moment. Mother and child gaze downwards, absorbed in the washing of small feet.

Before there were bathrooms and running water from taps, people used to pour water from a large jug into a wide china bowl to wash. Here the jug and the bowl are on the floor, so that the child can dip her toes in the water.

### Look closer

- Can you see a shadowy person in the doorway of the cottage in *The Naughty Boy*?
- When you look at *The Bath*, do you seem to be looking up at the two people or down at them?
- Can you find three different patterns in *The Bath* picture? Which part is not patterned?
- Which are the smoothest parts of the sculpture of the *Madonna and Child*?

The Child's Bath, by Mary Cassatt

### Activity

Make a splashy, watery painting of *you* being washed, showered or bathed. Show whether you enjoy it or not!

8

9

Under the 'Look Closer' heading there are questions for you to answer. They will help you to become really involved in what's going on in the pictures.

Where you see this hand sign, you will find an art 'Activity' to try on your own. Each one suggests ways in which you can use ideas in the artists' work in your own pictures.

At the end of the book there is a chance for you to be an art detective! You will find collections of details from many of the pictures. How sharp are your eyes? Can you find where the details come from?

# Mother and Child

The Naughty Boy,
*by Hubert von
Herkomer*

▲ A pretty country cottage, overgrown with roses and creepers, is the background for a family scene. An **angry** mother lifts up her *naughty* boy, and her head is turned away as she furiously tells someone behind her what he has done. The little boy looks uncomfortable as he is held roughly under the arms. Neither of them looks happy.

◀ The infant Jesus is **frightened** by a fluttering bird, which young St John holds out to him. He turns to his mother Mary for comfort. The scene is carved out of a stone called marble, but the artist did not finish it. Can you see where Michelangelo's chisel cut the stone *roughly* at the outer edges? He then used a smaller chisel to chip *d e l i c a t e l y* at the figures.

Madonna and Child,
*by Michelangelo Buonarroti*

▷ This artist loved to paint mothers with their children. She captured their most **tender** moments together. Bath-time is ordinary and everyday, yet here we feel that we are allowed to *p e e p* in on an especially private moment. Mother and child gaze downwards, absorbed in the washing of small feet.

Before there were bathrooms and running water from taps, people used to pour water from a large jug into a wide china bowl to wash. Here the jug and the bowl are on the floor, so that the child can dip her toes in the water.

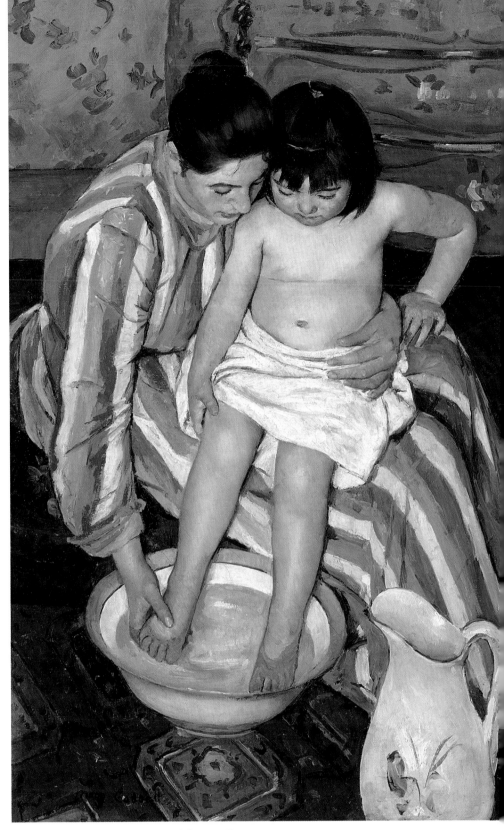

The Child's Bath, *by Mary Cassatt*

## Look closer

- Can you see a shadowy person in the doorway of the cottage in *The Naughty Boy*?

- When you look at *The Bath*, do you seem to be looking up at the two people or down at them?

- Can you find three different patterns in *The Bath* picture? Which part is not patterned?

- Which are the smoothest parts of the sculpture of the *Madonna and Child*?

## Activity

Make a splashy, watery painting of *you* being washed, showered or bathed. Show whether you enjoy it or not!

9

# Faces

Portrait of a Lady in Yellow,
*by Alesso Baldovinetti*

◀ A side view of a head like this is called a **profile** portrait. This picture is very obviously of a real person. Her pale and delicate face has a crisp, clear outline. The artist has paid great attention to *detail*. See how each strand of hair stands out against the blue background, and how boldly the black leaf design shows up on her yellow spotted sleeve.

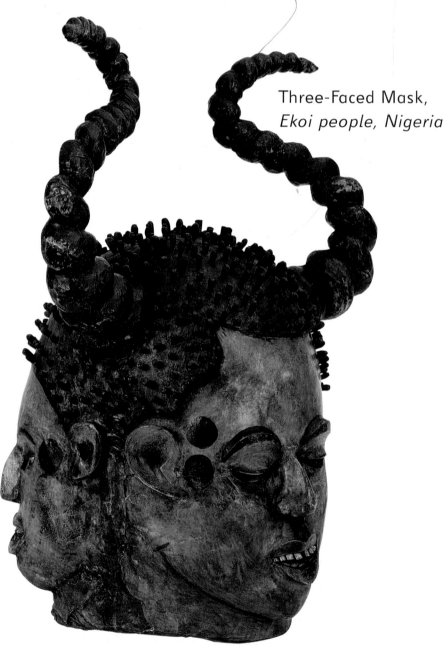

Three-Faced Mask,
*Ekoi people, Nigeria*

## Look closer

- Where else, in everyday things, can you see a head in profile?
- Can you find other carefully painted details in the profile portrait?
- How would you describe the different way that the two faces have been painted?
- Did you spot a sideways figure-of-eight shape in the picture by Klee?

▲ This is an **all-round view** of a head. It has a face on three sides. It can look in all directions at once, to see, hear and understand everything. Its three faces can also look into the past, the present and the future.

Senecio, *by Paul Klee*

▲ This is a **front view** of a face. It is made up of lots of different shapes. Can you find circles, rectangles, squares, ovals, and a triangle? This is also a portrait of a real person, but the artist has not tried to make his face look **realistic**. The person was a performer, who wore a multi-coloured costume called a *harlequin*. See how the shapes in the face are like the shapes in the harlequin costume.

## Activity

Draw a face using only circles, or using only squares or rectangles, or using only triangles. Then make a face with a mixture of shapes, and colour it in gorgeous colours.

# Figures

## Look closer

- Looking at all three pictures, which words would you use to describe which figure: slender, stiff, massive, rough-textured, weighty?
- The thin figure of the *Man Pointing* is made of a metal called bronze. Do you think it looks heavy?
- Why do you think the artist has not used many curves in the soldier painting?
- Can you find the figure of the Queen in *Trooping the Colour*? How has the artist made her look different from all the other figures?

Man Pointing,
*by Alberto Giacometti*

▶ This figure points with his right hand and seems to beckon with his left. When this artist modelled his figures he said that he looked for the "**bones under the skin**". This figure certainly looks thin and bony, like a stick man. His body is much longer than it would be in real life. This makes it look very *fragile*, as if it could break easily.

▶ The artist who made this drawing of a woman is famous for his sculptures. You can see how, even in this sketch, he is thinking of the figure as if it were a sculpture. Look at the way his pen strokes make her seem **solid**, rounded and as **HEAVY** as stone.

*Detail from* Draped Standing Figures, *by Henry Moore*

Trooping the Colour, *by William Roberts*

▲ Every year in London, soldiers carrying regimental flags (called "colours") march to celebrate the Queen's birthday. Here the Queen inspects the troops who have gathered in her honour. All the figures are **stiff** and **straight**. Guns, swords, arms, legs, flag-poles, and even trouser stripes, are all painted in *vertical* lines, to add to the strong and *upright* look of the scene.

▶ The men almost look as if they have been made by a machine, like toy soldiers.

## Activity

Use modelling clay to make some HEAVY, **stone-like** sculptures of people. Then, as a contrast, use pipe cleaners to make some *thin, wiry* people.

# Moving Figures

The Mud Bath, *by David Bomberg*

At first glance you might think that these shapes have *nothing* to do with people. Look carefully and you will see these are shapes of people **jostling** each other as they gather around a steam bath. This artist enjoyed the excitement and power of machines, and here the movements of the figures almost suggest parts of a *throbbing* machine at work.

## Look closer

- Can you find the shapes of people leaping and diving in *The Mud Bath*?

- Klee's figure does not look solid. How is the way he shows movement different from Bomberg's?

- The athlete is made of a hard shiny stone called marble. Can you imagine how difficult it was to carve this whole figure from one single block of stone?

▶ Paul Klee drew this **dancing** figure with one continuous long line, one squiggle, two dots and a dash! With your finger, follow the line all the way round and see how he did it. The picture is full of *energy* and **movement**.

## Activity

Take a line for a walk! Practice making the shape of a person without ever taking your pencil off the paper. This is a very good way to capture quick movements.

Discus Thrower,
*ancient Rome*

Tanzt Entsetzen,
*by Paul Klee*

◀ In ancient times Greek and Roman sculptors studied the way our muscles work, to make their figures look as lifelike as possible. It was a real challenge to show an athlete in this difficult pose. Look at how the shoulders and hips slope downwards, the legs point forwards, while the chest and head twist sideways, towards us. Yet the figure is perfectly **balanced**. *You* try to take up this tricky pose!

# Working

The Builders, *by Fernand Léger*

Look at the way the artist has used dots and stripes as a *pattern* in this picture.

◄ Large hands and strong muscles enable these builders to lift a massive iron girder into place on this building site. Look through the **hard**, straight lines of ladders and iron bars to the contrasting *s o f t* clouds floating in a clear sunny sky. Leger always liked to use really *bright* colours in his pictures.

## Activity

Make a pattern picture with
H O R I Z O N T A L and
V E R T I C A L
lines, like Leger's painting.
Add some **dots** and **stripes**,
and some diagonal lines, to make
your pattern really *exciting*.

Peasants Binding Faggots, *by Pieter Bruegel*

## Look closer

- The peasants collecting wood are looking watchful, perhaps slightly alarmed. Why do you think they are so alert?
- One of these pictures is 400 years old. Can you guess which one?
- Verbs are doing words, like *lift, carry, pull, push, collect*. Which of these verbs describe activities in which picture?

▲ In the *distance* a man chops thin branches of wood for the other two men to collect and tie into bundles. These twigs, or faggots, will be used as **kindling** wood to get a fire going.

▲ The large man is healthy and **strong**, while the thin man looks ill and ragged. Perhaps he has a painful toothache!

# Relaxing

Holiday, *by James Tissot*

▲ A group of elegantly dressed people are having
a picnic beside a garden pond, in the shade of a
horse-chestnut tree. They look very *r e l a x e d*,
sipping tea and resting against the trees or against
each other. Do you think the old lady has dozed off
with her cup of tea still in her hand? Tissot enjoyed
painting beautiful clothes, like the ones the people
are wearing in this picture. He painted this scene in
his own London garden.

## Activity

Make a drawing of four people in contrasting
poses. One should look E N E R G E T I C , one
should look **busy**, one should look *l a z y* and
one should look r e l a x e d . When you have
finished, ask someone if they can tell which
is which!

These young men are relaxing. One is *l a z i l y* swimming in a cool and shady pool, two are *gently* wrestling on the grass, and some are just **dreaming**. This picture was painted in the artist's studio, but the fresh daylight colours make you think it was painted outdoors. This is just what the artist wanted, to give the impression that he had actually been at the bathing scene.

## Look closer

- Look at the arrangement of the glass water bottles on the picnic cloth in *Holiday*. It echoes the shape of the horse-chestnut leaves above. What else is arranged like this?

- Can you find four men, three young women, one old lady and a child in *Holiday*? Look carefully — they aren't all easy to see!

- In which season was *Holiday* painted? How can you tell?

Summer Scene, by Jean Frédéric Bazille

# Animals

The Forest Fire, *by Piero di Cosimo*

▲ This painting shows a beautiful country scene on a lovely summer day – and yet something is **wrong**. Fire sweeps through the heart of the forest, while men and animals flee for their lives. Flames and sparks *l e a p* through the leaves, and smoke *billows* through the branches. The artist made this picture about 500 years ago. He wanted to make the animals and the countryside as important as the people in his paintings, to show that they are all part of the wonders of creation.

## Activity

With friends, make a l o n g picture based on this painting, to put up on the wall. Create a magical forest with paint, and cut out your animals from coloured or patterned paper to make a collage. Add as many animals as you like. Imagine and draw your own 'part animal, part human' creatures to live in this strange world.

#  Look closer

- How many different kinds of animal can you recognise?

- Can you find two strange creatures with animal bodies and human faces?

- Find four places where the forest is on fire.

- Why has the artist painted some animals and birds much smaller than others?

▶ You can clearly see the fear on this animal's face.

# Imagined Creatures

◀ This terrifying, imaginary monster is carved out of wood. It has a fierce expression with big **staring** eyes. It was part of a house doorpost, and may have been used to *frighten* away evil spirits.

▼ In China, where this picture was made, dragons are imagined as beautiful creatures who bring **good luck**. This dragon is embroidered on a royal robe in coloured silk thread. It is decorated with tiny pearls, called seed pearls. Chinese people perform a traditional dance to *honour* the dragon. The dance looks like the **twisting** shape of this dragon's body.

Figure from a House Post, *Maori, New Zealand*

Imperial Dragon, *China*

## Activity

Draw an amazing dream creature of your own. Think of the different sorts of imaginary beings, such as goblins, giants, pixies and other fairy people, monsters, serpents and half-human, half-animal creatures.

▶ A unicorn is an imaginary white horse with a single horn in the centre of its forehead. Here the swift, wild creature has been captured, fenced in, and tied to a tree with a chain and decorated collar. This is a *woven* picture, called a **tapestry**, which would have been used as a wall hanging in a castle or palace. Some, like this one, have the background covered with flowers. They are called *mille fleur* or 'thousand flower' tapestries.

The Unicorn in Captivity, *France*

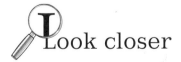 ook closer

- Can you see that the unicorn's horn is a spiral?
- Was the unicorn injured when it was captured?
- Do you think that the wooden Maori monster is laughing, glaring, pulling a rude face or just looking rather sad?
- How many sharp claws and teeth can you see on the Imperial Dragon?

# Spring and Summer

Spring, *by Frederick Walker*

▲ Two children gather primroses. The girl pushes aside *whippy* twigs of pussy willow to reach some hidden flowers. This picture was painted outdoors in spring, in very great **detail**. You can almost see each individual leaf. Although the artist planned the picture carefully, he wanted it to look as if he had **accidentally** captured this *charming* moment.

On a glorious day in the summer holidays, three of the artist's children are enjoying an idle morning in a rowing boat. Elizabeth, Sylvia and George are *dangling* lines into the sea and waiting patiently to catch some fish. The bright light *shimmers* off the water in the **h e a t** of the sun?

## Look closer

- What colours has the artist used to make the shadows in *Calm Morning*?

- Look at the boats. Do you think there is enough breeze for them to sail?

- How many different colours and textures can you find in *Spring*? Notice that the ground is much more than just a plain green carpet of grass.

- Why does the weather look hotter in *Calm Morning* than it does in *Spring*?

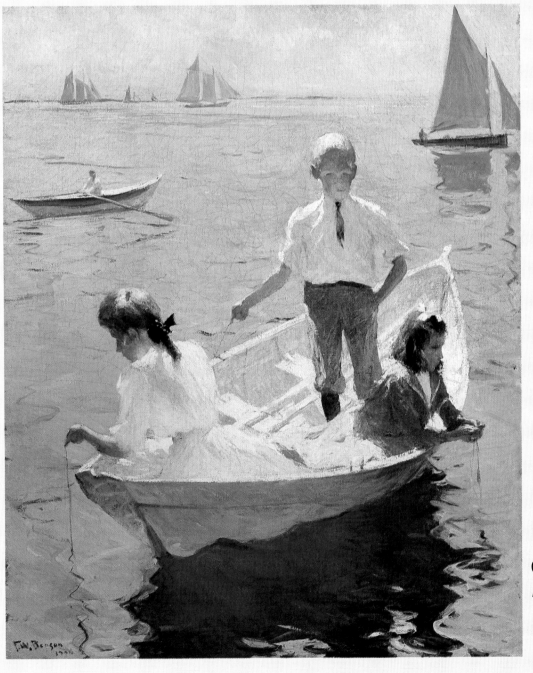

## Activity

Make a picture of boats with their reflections mirrored in the water, like the sailing boats in *Calm Morning*. Choose warm, bright colours for a summer scene and pale, fresh colours for a spring scene.

Calm Morning,
*by Frank Weston Benson*

# Autumn and Winter

Autumn Leaves, *by John Everett Millais*

The artist Millais said he wanted to paint a picture 'full of beauty'. He chose this glowing autumn scene, in a garden in Scotland. The distant hills look almost purple in the twilight, as Alice, Sophie, Mattie and Isobella heap the **red-gold** leaves ready for a bonfire. You can almost *smell* burning leaves when you look at this picture.

## Activity

Mix rich, deep warm colours for an autumn picture. You could even stick on some real autumn leaves in beautiful colours and shapes, and paint in coloured berries and seeds. Mix cool blues and greys for a winter calendar picture. Make it look so icy that it makes you *shiver* !

October.
*From 'Les très riches heures du Duc de Berry'*

In this autumn picture farmers are busy sowing seeds for a crop in the spring. The horse pulls a harrow to break up the **hard** earth into neat rows. The man in blue *scatters* seed by hand.

A Winter's Scene, *by David Teniers*

▲ **Frozen** fields meant that little farm work could be done in winter, so people had time to enjoy skating, sledging and games in the snow. Food was *s c a r c e*, so the killing of the household pig, shown here, was an important family event. It gave them delicious fresh meat, pies and sausages to last for months.

▶ The woman with the long-handled pan is waiting to catch the pig's blood. Boys holding straws wait to **burn** the tough hairs off its skin.

## Look closer

- The winter scene is painted in *silvery* grey colours, the autumn picture in rich, **glowing** colours. How does each picture make you feel?

- At what time of day do you think that the children are collecting autumn leaves?

- The man in the middle of the *October* picture is actually a scarecrow. Do you think the birds are frightened by his bow and arrow?

# Light and Shade

The Starry Night, *by Vincent van Gogh*

▼ Van Gogh was an unhappy and lonely man, but his pictures are full of *energy* and **joy**. Look at the moon detail. See how **thick** the paint is and how *excited* the brushstrokes are. They show colour, texture and pattern all together.

▲ It is night, and the lights are on in the houses of this French village. Above, the deep blue sky **glows** with brilliant stars *w h i r l i n g* in space. This grand sky makes the dark village look tiny. The tree and the church spire link the earth with the heavens.

Lady Osuma and Sasaya Hanbei, *by Shunkosai Hokuei*

◄ These two people are actors in a play. The angry Lady Osuna has been hiding in a cave, waiting to **jump** out and *surprise* the villain of the plot. He looks guilty. The *contrast* is strong between the light from the torch and the surrounding darkness.

The Fighting Temeraire, *by William Turner*

'The Fighting Temeraire' was a sailing **warship**. It looks *g h o s t l y* in the sunset. This is a sad scene because the ship is now too old to be useful in battle, and so a tug boat is pulling it along the River Thames to be broken up.

## Look closer

- Which picture shows sunlight, firelight and reflected light?
- Which picture shows starlight and moonlight?
- How have Van Gogh and Turner painted the sky differently?
- What do you think the angry Japanese lady is saying?
  Can *you* make the expressions on the actors' faces?

Turner painted with brushes, but he also put paint on with a knife, rags, the ends of his brushes and even with his *hands*!

## Activity

Make your own colourful sunset or starry moonlight picture using **THICK** brushstrokes. Experiment with ways to add on paint, like Turner did. Remember to wash your brushes often to keep your colours clear.

# Music

The Banjo Lesson, *by Henry Ossawa Tanner*

▲ A boy concentrates on **plucking** the right string on his banjo. It is not easy for him, because he is small and the banjo seems very large. This is probably a father and son together. They seem close and loving, as they share the music lesson in their warm and *homely* kitchen. Look at how the **texture** of the paint in the background gives a lively and interesting feel to the plain walls.

## Look closer

- How has the artist made the plain and simple kitchen in the *Banjo Lesson* look so cosy?

- In *The Harpsichord Lesson* there are lots of carefully painted details, like the man's earring and his belt-buckle. Can you find any others?

- Look at the long, thin horn the angel Gabriel is blowing. What sort of sound do you think he is making?

## Activity

Listen to a piece of music. What sort of ideas and pictures come into your head? Make a picture of the music. It does not have to look like anything you recognise.

The Harpsichord Lesson, *by Jan Steen*

▲ A pretty girl is working hard at her music lesson. She is playing a **harpsichord**, which is an early sort of piano. She is being watched carefully by her teacher, who is pointing to her fingers. This is an ordinary household scene, but the artist has painted it in great detail. He has used a *delicate* and *gentle* colour scheme.

◀ The angel Gabriel delivers a musical **fanfare** to announce good news sent from God to mankind. Gabriel strides along purposefully. The feeling of movement and rhythm is made stronger by his *flowing* wings, floating sashes and *flying* hat-trim.

Angel Gabriel, *Egypt or Syria*

# Dance

▶ It is night and people are dancing by moonlight beside the sea. The artist has painted the place where she grew up, in Portugal. Memories from her childhood often come into her pictures. This picture is a 'dance of life'. At first a young girl is alone, then she dances with the man she will marry, and then she dances while she is pregnant with her own child. The three figures dancing in the background show 'the three ages of woman'.

## Activity

Roll out modelling clay into thin strips. On a flat surface make the rubbery strips into people *dancing*. You can make exaggerated poses easily and change anything in seconds, just as poses change in a dance.

The Dance, *by Paula Rego*

Shield Dance, *by Spencer Asah, Native American*

◀ This scene is not as **fierce** as it looks! These members of the Kiowa tribe of Native Americans are acting out a war scene in a dance. These sorts of dances have become a traditional and proud **celebration** of the way they once used to live.

- Can you guess at a name for the Native American chiefs by looking at their shields?

- See how the long hair of the Indian god makes a pattern as it floats with the rhythm of the dance.

- How does the artist show that the figures in *The Dance* are dancing, and not standing still?

▶ This sculpture shows the Hindu god, Shiva Nataraja, dancing in a circle of fire. He gracefully lifts one foot, while crushing a wicked demon with the other. The flames *flickering* around the outside circle look like his fingers twisting and turning as he dances. His many arms create a feeling of movement and **rhythm**. It is not surprising he is also known as the Lord of the Dance.

Shiva Nataraja, *India*

33

# Shapes

Swinging,
*by Wassily
Kandinsky*

◀ This picture does not look like anything that we can *recognise* in real life. The artist wanted his glowing colours and beautiful shapes to make us think about our feelings. He believed **feelings** were as important a subject for paintings as the things we see around us.

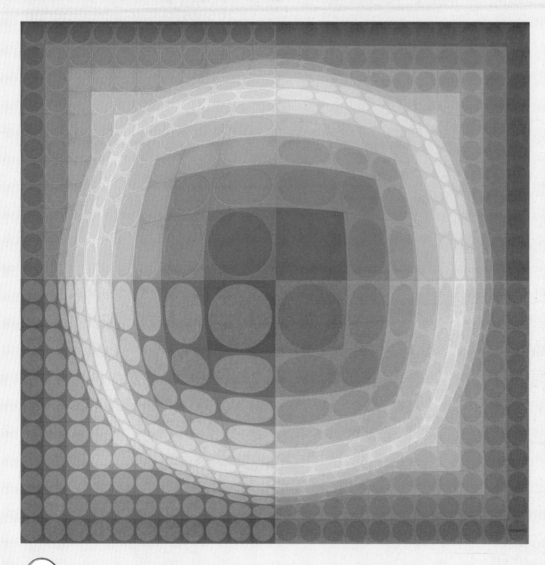

◀ This artist liked to paint pictures that can *trick your eye*. The painting is on a flat surface, yet by cleverly arranging the shapes and colours he makes you think the picture is **bulging** in the middle. The design of the picture is perfectly **symmetrical**. This means that the shapes are *identical* on both sides of an invisible line through the centre.

Pal-Ket, *by Victor Vasarély*

## Look closer

- In *Swinging*, how many rectangles, circles, half circles and triangles can you find?
- Is there a perfect square in *Swinging*?
- What is the effect of *Pal-Ket* on your eyes? Does the picture seem to be moving?
- Can you see how the artist has squashed some of the circles in *Pal-Ket*? Why do you think he has done this?

## Activity

Make a perfectly balanced pattern by painting a design on only half your sheet of paper. Before the paint dries, fold the paper over so that the design prints on the empty half of the paper. You will then have a **symmetrical** painting!

# Patterns

Expectation, *by Gustav Klimt*

◀ The woman in this painting looks mysterious. She is nearly hidden by the **bold** pattern of her clothes and the swirling, curving design of the background. Only her face and hands can be seen as she *gazes* out of the picture looking for some*one* or some*thing*. Klimt made his pictures look like brilliantly coloured **mosaics**. He loved to use gleaming gold and silver, perhaps because his father was a silversmith who made designs in precious metals.

## Activity

Make a mosaic collage. Cut up lots of small pieces of brightly coloured paper, perhaps from magazines, and stick them on to some paper in a patterned design. Add sequins and dots of gleaming glitter-glue for extra shine.

Australian Aboriginal artists used to tell stories about their homeland in sand pictures. This painting uses patterns to show the desert, as if you were looking down on it from above. Circles may be water holes, wavy lines may be rivers or snakes, routes are marked by animal tracks. It may also be a picture of 'Dreamtime', which is the Aborigines' way of explaining how the world began.

Possum, Wallaby and Cockatoo Dreaming, *by Michael Jagamara Nelson*

This royal portrait has rich patterns of precious **jewels** and fine **embroidery**, which show the queen's wealth and importance. Her dress is covered with pearls and rubies in a complicated design. It is very *intricate* and would have been very heavy to wear.

# Look closer

- How many different textures can you find in the portrait of Elizabeth I?
- The rose in the top left corner of the portrait of Elizabeth I is repeated on her dress. Can you find it?
- Can you find hidden in the desert patterns the tracks for the wallaby, the possum and the cockatoo?
- Can you find the eyes hidden in the pattern of the woman's dress in *Expectation*?

Elizabeth I, *by Nicholas Hilliard*

# Letters

One aeroplane shoots another down in flames – whaam! The artist took the idea for this picture from a comic, because he wanted to create the excitement and energy of a **cartoon**. He has even included a speech bubble. The picture is *huge*, the size of a whole wall in a small room. The strong design and startling bright colours make it an extraordinarily powerful picture.

Whaam!, *by Roy Lichtenstein*

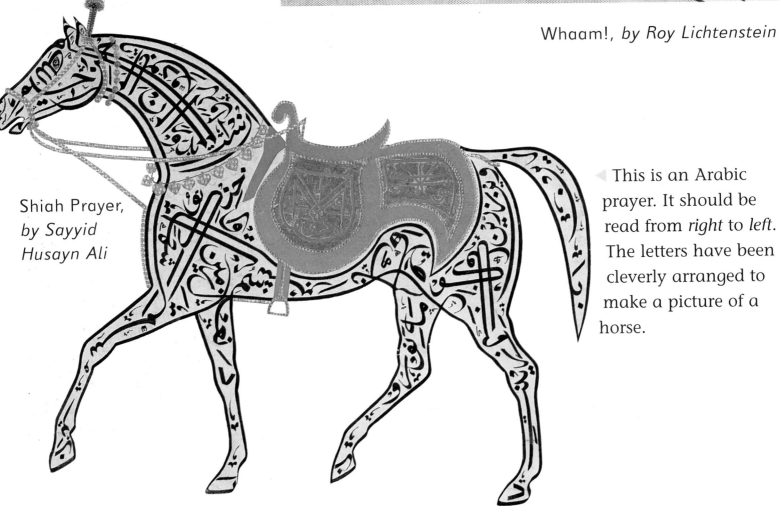

Shiah Prayer, *by Sayyid Husayn Ali*

This is an Arabic prayer. It should be read from *right* to *left*. The letters have been cleverly arranged to make a picture of a horse.

## Activity

Draw an **action-packed** picture, with people having a conversation in speech bubbles. Make the words L A R G E and important in the picture.

▼ Letters are **dotted** around in a lively background pattern, on this page from a book. The book contains prayers and bible readings, decorated with beautiful pictures, and was made by *hand* for a lady called Marguerite d'Orléans to use when she prayed alone at home. It is called a 'Book of Hours'.

## Look closer

- Look closely at the background of *Whaam!* Can you see that it is made up of large painted dots? This it to make it look as if it has been printed on a machine.

- In *Whaam!* the shapes are heavily outlined in black. Why do you think the artist has done this?

- Trace the outlines of the horse with your finger. Every line turns into an Arabic letter.

- Long ago quill pens, made from large feathers, were used for writing, and so letters looked different from ours today. Can you recognise all the letters in this book detail?

Heures de Marguerite d'Orléans, *France*

39

# That's Strange

Golconda, *by René Magritte*

Here is a perfectly ordinary street in daytime. But something very odd is happening. From a cloudless blue sky it is raining the strangest rain! The artist has painted things to look as real as possible, but he has added something quite unreal and *impossible*. This reminds us how important are our *dreams* and **imagination**.

## Look closer

- The 'raining men' above are all dressed in the same way. What do you think their work could be?

- Notice the countryside seen through the window next to the grandfather. Do you think the artist has copied it from real life, or imagined it?

- The sculpture has interesting shaped holes. Do they make the figure look heavier or lighter? Why?

A grandfather has his arms round his grandson, whose small hand tenderly reaches up to him. The old man looks large and **solid**, while the child seems small and *delicate*. His long wavy hair looks odd to us, but when the picture was painted, about 500 years ago, this was how young boys looked. The strange bumps on the grandfather's face are a skin problem of old age, called 'potato nose'. The cracks on his forehead are just splits in the paint.

## Activity

Ghirlandaio painted his picture with 'tempera' paint. This is powder colour mixed with egg yolk, to make a creamy, very shiny paint that lasts a long time. Try making a small picture using this mixture – but watch out, it dries hard as a rock in minutes!

Portrait of an Old Man with a Young Boy
*by Domenico Ghirlandaio*

Look carefully at this sculpture and you will see the shape of a woman lying back in a relaxed pose. The artist was fascinated by the shapes of **caves** in hillsides and cliffs, and he made his sculptures of women seem to be part of the *landscape*. He thought the spaces were as interesting as the solid parts.

Reclining Figure, 1951, *by Henry Moore*

# Art Detective Quiz

You have now looked at lots of different pictures – but how well do you **remember** them? Be a Picture Detective. Try this quiz to find out how *sharp* your eyes are. When you've done the quiz yourself, you could try it out on an adult, to test how observant *they* are!

Are you good at remembering faces? Look back through the pictures to match each of these details to the right painting.

## Find the Faces!

A portrait is a painting of a real person, not an imagined one. The many portrait faces in this book all have different expressions. Which did you like best? What would your favourite face be saying, if it could speak?

## Find the Hands!

Where have you seen these hands before? Look back through the pictures in the book to find out whose they are.

Did you know that even when you are not talking, your hands can give messages to other people, for example when you point, clap, or wave.

How many different kinds of hand gesture can you find in the pictures?

# Find the Backgrounds!

Did you notice what was happening in the background of any of the paintings in this book? Let your eye 'travel' around a picture, to look at every single thing the artist has painted. That way, you won't miss anything important.

**Which paintings do these background details come from?**

# Find the Hidden Patterns!

Pattern is all around you. If you look carefully you will see patterns in almost all the works of art in this book. Sometimes it is made by the thickly painted brushstrokes, or by the texture of a carving or a sculpture. Perhaps it is the pattern of leaves against the sky, or the folds of someone's clothes.

**Which pictures do these pattern details come from? How many more patterns can you find?**

# Picture List

This list tells you when each picture was made, what size it is, who the artist was and what materials they used. It also tells you in which gallery or museum in the world you can see it.

## Mother and Child

**p.8 *The Naughty Boy,* 1888**
HUBERT VON HERKOMER
oil on canvas 158 x 235 cm
*Watford Borough Council Museum*

**p.8 *Madonna and Child with the Infant St John (The Taddei Tondo),* 1504**
MICHELANGELO BUONARROTI
Carrara marble relief
104 x 106.5 cm
*Royal Academy of Arts, London*

**p.9 *The Child's Bath,* 1893**
MARY CASSATT
oil on canvas
100.33 x 66 cm
*The Art Institute of Chicago, Robert A. Waller Fund*

## Faces

**p.10 *Portrait of a Lady in Yellow,* c.1465**
ALESSO BALDOVINETTI
tempera and oil on wood
62.9 x 40.6 cm
*National Gallery, London*

**p.10 *Three-Faced Mask***
NIGERIAN MASK, EKOI
*Deutsches Leder Museum, Frankfurt*

**p.11 *Senecio,* 1922**
PAUL KLEE
oil on gauze on cardboard
40.5 x 38 cm
*Oeffentliche Kunstsammlung Basel*

## Figures

**p.12 *Man Pointing,* 1947**
ALBERTO GIACOMETTI
bronze
176.5 x 90 x 62 cm
*Tate Gallery, London*

**p.12 Detail from *Draped Standing Figures in Red,* 1948**
HENRY MOORE
crayon, ink and wash
29.2 x 24.1 cm
*Private Collection, USA*

**p.13 *Trooping the Colour,* 1958-9**
WILLIAM ROBERTS
oil on canvas
183 x 274 cm
*Tate Gallery, London*

## Moving Figures

**p.14 *The Mud Bath,* 1914**
DAVID BOMBERG
oil on canvas
152.5 x 224 cm
*Tate Gallery, London*

**p.15 *Discus Thrower,* 2nd century**
GRAECO-ROMAN
marble
height 1650 cm
*Townley Collection, British Museum, London*

**p.15 *Tanzt Entsetzen,* 1931**
PAUL KLEE
pen and coloured ink
47.9 x 31.4 cm
*Museum of Fine Arts, Boston, Gift of Mr and Mrs Richard K. Weil*

## Working

**p.16 *The Builders,* 1950**
FERNAND LÉGER
oil on canvas
299.8 x 200 cm
*Musée National Fernand Léger, Biot, Gift of Nadia Léger and Georges Bauquier*

**p.17 *Two Peasants Binding Faggots,* 1500s**
PIETER BRUEGEL
oil on wood
36.2 x 27.3 cm
*Barber Institute of Fine Arts, University of Birmingham, Edgebaston*

## Relaxing

**p.18 *Holiday,* c.1876**
JAMES TISSOT
oil on canvas
76.2 x 99.4 cm
*Tate Gallery, London*

**p.19 *Summer Scene,* 1869**
JEAN FRÉDÉRIC BAZILLE
oil on canvas
160.02 x 160.66 cm
*Courtesy of the Fogg Art Museum, Harvard University Art Museums, Gift of Mr and Mrs F. Meynier de Salinelles*

## Animals

p.20 *The Forest Fire*, 1480s
PIERO DI COSIMO
oil on panel
71 x 203 cm
*Ashmolean Museum, Oxford*

## Imagined Creatures

p.22 *Figure from a House Post*, early 19th century
MAORI, NEW ZEALAND
wood
height 109.22 cm
*The Metropolitan Museum of Art, New York, The Michael C. Rockefeller Memorial Collection, Bequest of Nelson A. Rockefeller, 1979*

p.22 *Robe, 'Dragon and flaming pearl'*
CHINESE, CH'ING DYNASTY, T'UNG PERIOD (1862-74)
satin embroidered in silks, seed pearls and coral; couched in gold and silver
*The Metropolitan Museum of Art, New York, Gift of Robert E. Tod, 1929*

p.23 *The Unicorn in Captivity*, c.1500
FRANCO-FLEMISH: 'THE UNICORN TAPESTRIES'
silk, wool, silver and silver-gilt threads
368.3 x 243.84 x 7.62 cm
*The Metropolitan Museum of Art, New York, Gift of John D. Rockefeller Jr, The Cloisters Collection, 1937*

## Spring and Summer

p.24 *Spring*, 1864
FREDERICK WALKER
watercolour and bodycolour
62.2 x 50.2 cm
*Victoria and Albert Museum, London*

p.25 *Calm Morning*, 1904
FRANK WESTON BENSON
oil on canvas
112.7 x 91.8 cm
*Museum of Fine Arts, Boston, Gift of Charles A. Coolidge Family*

## Autumn and Winter

p.26 *Autumn Leaves*, 1855-6
JOHN EVERETT MILLAIS
oil on canvas
104.1 x 73.6 cm
*Manchester City Art Galleries*

p.26 *October*, from *Les Très Riches Heures du Duc de Berry*, c.1410
FRENCH MANUSCRIPT
whole sheet 22.2 x 13.5 cm
*Musée Condé, Chantilly*

p.27 *A Winter's Scene*, 1600s
DAVID TENIERS
oil on canvas
68 x 94 cm
*Dulwich Picture Gallery, London*

## Light and Shade

p.28 *The Starry Night*, 1889
VINCENT VAN GOGH
oil on canvas
73.7 x 92.1 cm
*Museum of Modern Art, New York. Acquired through the Lillie P. Bliss Bequest*

p.28 *Lady Osuna and Sasaya Hanbei*, 1836
SHUNKOSAI HOKUEI
woodblock print
37.2 x 50.5 cm
*Victoria and Albert Museum, London*

p.29 *The Fighting 'Temeraire' tugged to her last Berth to be broken up*, 1838
JOSEPH MALLORD WILLIAM TURNER
oil on canvas
90.8 x 121.9 cm
*National Gallery, London*

## Music

p.30 *The Banjo Lesson*, 1893
HENRY OSSAWA TANNER
oil on canvas
124.6 x 90.17 cm
*Hampton University Museum, Hampton, Virginia*

p.31 *The Harpsichord Lesson*, 1660s
JAN STEEN
oil on panel
36.5 x 48.3 cm
*Wallace Collection, London*

p.31 *Angel Gabriel, Wonders of Creation*
ISLAMIC MANUSCRIPT FROM EGYPT OR SYRIA
38.3 x 24.8 cm
*British Museum, London*

## Dance

p.32 *The Dance,* 1988
PAULA REGO
acrylic on paper laid
on canvas
213.4 x 274.3 cm
*Tate Gallery, London*

p.32 *Shield Dance,* c.1930
SPENCER ASAH, KIOWA
*US Department of the Interior,
Indian Arts and Crafts Board,
Southern Plains Indian Museum*

p.33 *Shiva as Nataraja [Lord
of the Dance],* 19th-20th
century
SOUTHERN INDIA
bronze
78 x 66 cm
*Oriental Museum, Durham
University*

## Shapes

p.34 *Swinging,* 1925
WASSILY KANDINSKY
oil on board
70.5 x 50.2 cm
*Tate Gallery, London*

p.35 *Pal-Ket,* 1973-4
VICTOR VASARÉLY
acrylic on canvas
151.2 x 150.8 cm
*Museo de Bellas Artes, Bilbao*

## Patterns

p.36 *Expectation,* 1905-9
GUSTAV KLIMT
cartoon for a section of the
Stoclet Frieze: tempera,
watercolour and gold paint
on paper
193 x 115 cm
*Palais Stoclet, Brussels*

p.37 *Possum, Wallaby and
Cockatoo Dreaming,* 1984
MICHAEL JAGAMARA NELSON
synthetic polymer paint on
canvas
102 x 121 cm
*National Gallery of Australia,
Canberra*

p.37 *Queen Elizabeth I
– The Pelican Portrait,* c.1572
ATTRIBUTED TO NICHOLAS
HILLIARD
oil on panel
76.8 x 59.7 cm
*Walker Art Gallery, Liverpool*

## Letters

p.38 *Whaam!,* 1963
ROY LICHTENSTEIN
acrylic on canvas
172.7 x 406.4 cm
*Tate Gallery, London*

p.38 *Sh'iah Prayer in
Naskshi [Tugra in the form of
a Horse],* Lahore, late 19th
century
SAYYID HUSAYN ALI
28.6 x 36.7 cm
gouache and gilt on paper
*Victoria and Albert Museum,
London*

p.39 Detail from the *Heures
de Marguerite d'Orléans,*
c.1430
FRENCH MANUSCRIPT
paint on vellum
*Bibliothèque Nationale de
France, Paris*

## That's Strange

p.40 *Golconda,* 1953
RENÉ MAGRITTE
oil on canvas
80 x 100 cm
*Menil Collection, Houston*

p.41 *Portrait of an Old
Man with a Young Boy,* 1400s
DOMENICO GHIRLANDAIO
egg tempera
63 x 46 cm
*Musée du Louvre, Paris*

p.41 *Reclining Figure,* 1951
HENRY MOORE
plaster
105.5 x 227 x 89 cm
*Tate Gallery, London*

## Cover Images

*front cover*
*The Snail,* 1953
HENRI MATISSE
gouache on paper
286.4 x 287 cm
*Tate Gallery, London*

*back cover*
*Mrs Moody and her
Two Children,*
THOMAS GAINSBOROUGH
oil on canvas
233 x 152 cm
*Dulwich Picture Gallery, London*

*A Young Man,* c.1500
PIERO DI COSIMO
egg tempera on wood panel
38 x 41 cm
*Dulwich Picture Gallery, London*

*page 3*
*Monet in his Floating
Studio,* 1874
EDOUARD MANET
oil on canvas
80 x 98 cm
*Neue Pinakothek, Munich*

# Index

## A

Aboriginal Australian art 37
African art 10
Angel Gabriel 30-31
animals 20-23, 27, 37, 38
Asah, Spencer 32
*Autumn Leaves* 26-27

## B

Baldovinetti, Alesso 10
*Banjo Lesson, The* 30
*Bath, The* 9
Bazille, Jean Frédéric 19
Benson, Frank Weston 25
boats 25, 29
Bomberg, David 14
*Books of Hours* 26, 39
Bruegel, Pieter 17
*Builders, The* 16-17

## C

*Calm Morning* 25
cartoons 38
carving 8, 22
Cassatt, Mary 9
children 8-9, 24, 25, 26, 27, 30
Chinese art 22-23

## D

dance 15, 32-33
*Dance, The* 32-33
*Discus Thrower* 14-15
dragons 22-23
drawings 12, 15

## E

Ekoi tribe 10
*Elizabeth I* 37
embroidery 22, 37
*Expectation* 36-37

## F

faces 10-11
*Fighting Temeraire, The* 29
figures 12-19, 32-33, 41
fire 20-21, 29, 33
flowers 8, 23, 24
*Forest Fire, The* 20-21

## G

Ghirlandaio, Domenico 40-41
Giacometti, Alberto 12
*Golconda* 40
Greek art 15

## H

harlequin 11
*Harpsichord Lesson, The* 30-31
heads 10-11
Herkomer, Hubert von 8-9
*Heures de Marguerite d'Orléans* 39
Hilliard, Nicholas 37
Hokuei, Shunkosai 28-29
*Holiday* 18-19

## I

imagination 20, 22-23, 40-41
*Imperial Dragon* 22-23
Indian art 33
Islamic art 31, 38

## J

Japanese art 28-29

## K

Kandinsky, Wassily 34-35
Klee, Paul 10-11, 14-15
Klimt, Gustav 36-37

## L

*Lady Osuma and Sasaya Hanbei* 28-29
Léger, Fernand 16-17
letters 31, 38-39
Lichtenstein, Roy 38-39

## M

*Madonna and Child* 8-9
Magritte, René 40
*Man Pointing* 12
Maori art 22-23
marble 8, 14
Michelangelo Buonarroti 8
Millais, John Everett 26-27
mille fleur 23
monsters 22-23
Moore, Henry 12, 40-41
mosaics 36
mother and child 8-9
movement 14-15, 32-33
*Mud Bath, The* 14
music 30-31

## N

Native American art 32
*Naughty Boy, The* 8-9
Nelson, Michael Jagamarra 37

## P

*Pal-Ket* 35
pattern 9, 16-17, 36-37
*Peasants Binding Faggots* 17
Piero di Cosimo 20-21
*Portrait of an Old Man with a Young Boy* 40-41
*Portrait of a Lady in Yellow* 10
portraits 10, 37, 41
*Possum, Wallaby and Cockatoo Dreaming* 37
profiles 10

## R

realistic pictures 11
Rego, Paula 32-33
relaxing 18-19
rhythm 33
Roberts, William 12-13
Roman art 15

## S

sailing ship 29
Sayyid Husayn Ali 38
scarecrow 26-27
sculptures 12, 15, 40-41
seasons 19, 24-27
*Senecio* 10-11
shapes 34-35
*Shiva Nataraja* 33
snow 27
*Spring* 24-25

*Starry, The Night* 28-29
Steen, Jan 30-31
stone 8, 14
summer 19, 25
*Summer Scene* 19
sunlight 19, 25, 29
*Swinging* 34-35
symmetrical pictures 35

## T

Tanner, Henry Ossawa 30
*Tanzt Entsetzen* 14-15
tapestries 23
Teniers, David 27
Tissot, James 18-19
trees 17, 18, 19, 20-21, 23, 24
*Très riches heures du Duc de Berry, Les* 26-27
*Trooping the Colour* 12-13
Turner, William 29

## U

unicorn 23

## V

Van Gogh, Vincent 28-29
Vasarely, Victor 35

## W

Walker, Frederick 24
water 9, 18, 19, 25
weaving 23
*Whaam!* 38-39
*Winter's Scene, A* 27
wood 22, 41
working 16-17

# Acknowledgements

Licenced by the Aboriginal Artists' Agency/ National Gallery of Australia, Canberra: p 37t purchased with admission charges

Ashmolean Museum, Oxford: p 20-21

Photo Bibliothèque nationale de France, Paris: p 39b

Courtesy of the Museum of Fine Arts Boston: p15tr Klee © DACS, London 1999, p 25 & p 6bl

The Bridgeman Art Library, London: title page, p 16 Léger © ADAGP, Paris and DACS, London 1999, p 17, p 19, p 24, p 26tl, p 26br, p 31t, p 35 Vasarély © ADAGP, Paris and DACS, London 1999, p 33br, p 37b, p 40 Magritte © ADAGP, Paris and DACS, London 1999, p 41t

© The British Museum: p 15bl, p 31b

Photograph © 1998, The Art Institute of Chicago. All Rights Reserved: p 9 & p 7tr Cassatt: Robert A. Waller Fund 1910.2.

Dulwich Picture Gallery, London: back cover, p 27

Deutsches Ledermuseum, Frankfurt: p 10b

Hampton University Museum, Hampton, Virginia: p 30

By kind permission of Paula Rego and Marlborough Fine Art (London) Ltd: p 32

The Metropolitan Museum of Art, New York: p 22 & p 6r The Michael C.Rockefeller Memorial Collection, Bequest of Nelson A. Rockefeller 1979 (1979.206.1508)/Photograph © 1994 The Metropolitan Museum of Art, p 22br Gift of Robert E.Tod, 1929

(29.36)/Photograph © 1980 The Metropolitan Museum of Art, p 23 Gift of John D. Rockefeller, Jr., The Cloisters Collection 1937 (37.80.6)/Photograph © 1993 The Metropolitan Museum of Art

By permission of the Henry Moore Foundation, Hertfordshire: p 12r (HMF 2439), p 41b

The National Gallery, London/Corbis: p 10t, p 29

© 1999 The Museum of Modern Art, New York: p 28 tl and detail p 28 cr

Photo Offentliche Kunstsammlung Basel, Martin Bühler: p 11 Klee © DACS, London 1999

Royal Academy of Arts, London: p 8b & p 6tl & p 7cl

Tate Gallery, London: front cover Matisse © Succession H.Matisse/DACS, London 1999, p 12l Giacometti © ADAGP, Paris and DACS, London 1999, p 13 © Tate Gallery, London, p 18, p 34 Kandinsky © ADAGP, Paris and DACS, London 1999, p 38t © Estate of Roy Lichtenstein/ DACS, London 1999

Photo courtesy of the US Department of the Interior, Indian Arts and Crafts Board, Southern Plains Indian Museum: p 32bl

Victoria and Albert Museum, London V&A Picture Library: p 28bl, p 38b

Watford Borough Council Museum/Photo A.A.Barnes: p 8 & p 7tl